NATIONAL GEOGRAPHIC

D0503562

How Does My Bike Work?

Jan McPherson

I am riding my bike.
Look at how my bike works.

I push down on one pedal.
I push down on the other pedal.
I make the pedals go around.

When I make the pedals go around, they turn a big sprocket.

When the big sprocket goes around, it turns the chain.

When the chain goes around,
it turns a small sprocket.

When the small sprocket goes around,
it turns the back wheel.
When the back wheel goes around,
my bike moves forward.

When I need to turn,
I turn the handlebars.

When I turn the handlebars,
the front wheel turns.
My bike turns.

When I squeeze the brake lever,
the brake pads press against the tires.
My bike slows down.

This is how my bike works.

Glossary

brake lever	small bar on handlebars that operates the brake pad
brake pad	pad that presses against the tire to slow down the bike
chain	metal links joined together
handlebars	metal bar with handles that steers the bike
pedals	levers pressed by the feet to operate the bike
sprocket	circle of metal teeth that fits into a chain
tire	covering around a wheel
wheel	round object that turns